C000319863

my mother said

my mother said

RYLAND
PETERS
& SMALL

LONDON NEW YORK

Designer **Luana Gobbo**

Senior editor **Henrietta Heald**

Picture research **Emily Westlake**

Production **Susannah Straughan**

Art director **Gabriella Le Grazie**

Publishing director **Alison Starling**

First published in the United Kingdom in 2005 by
Ryland Peters & Small
20–21 Jockey's Fields
London WC1R 4BW
www.rylandpeters.com

ISBN 1 84172 844 6

Printed and bound in China.

contents

my mother said...

IT'S a known fact that many women become their mothers. We may spend our childhood and teenage years trying not to do what our mothers say, but in the end those precious seeds of wisdom take root, and before we know it we find ourselves saying the same things to our daughters — often in the same tone of voice.

Apart from the traditional gems of advice that generations of mothers have passed on to their children (of the 'Do as you would be done by' school), most of the wise remarks reproduced in this book are new – though the thoughts behind them are often familiar. We rely on our mothers to help us to cope with the wide world beyond the security of the childhood home, and many of the fragments of mothers' wisdom recalled here explore this ground. But it's also the little things that our mothers said — 'No, you can't have another biscuit', 'You'll have someone's eye out with that stick', 'You'll grow into it' — that underpin our memories of childhood.

We'd like to say a big thank you to all the daughters who spoke to us for the book — and, especially, to their mothers for being so wise.

Oh, what a power
is motherhood.

EURIPIDES

life

MY mother
taught me how to live
my own life.

'DON'T be apathetic or
settle for mediocrity. Always find
a passion, something to get excited
or enthusiastic about.'

I would say, 'That's not fair,'
and my mother would say,
'But life isn't fair.'

'RULES for a happy life:
be positive, be organized, and always
take your make-up off at night.'

'SEW, don't pin.'

'LIFE just gets better as you get older.'

'ADD a pinch of love to
everything that you do. It makes
life taste sweeter.'

'LIVE life to the full'.

MY mother taught me to be independent,
both financially and emotionally, for
which I am very grateful, and to be brave.
If my mother ever complains, you know
something is seriously wrong!

*Friendship is a serious affection;
the most sublime of all affections,
because it is founded on
principle, and cemented by time.*

MARY WOLLSTONECRAFT

other
people

'FRIENDS are very important. Look after your friends and they will look after you.'

'NEVER take the people closest to you for granted. Always let them know they are appreciated.'

'WHATEVER else you do, never be knowingly cruel or unkind.'

other people

WHEN my children became impatient
with a task or a person, I would say to them,
'It's easier to catch flies with honey than it is
with vinegar.' My mother told me the same
thing, and it helped me to slow down and
think carefully before speaking, rather
than blurting something out.

MY mother taught me to be kind
and compassionate, and to treat others
as I would like to be treated myself.

ONE of my mother's many qualities is her strong sense of justice and fairness. For instance, she has always been careful not to favour me over my younger brother, Christian, or vice versa, sometimes to an extreme degree. We were both given first names with nine letters; if I got some pocket money for sweets, he would get the same amount; if he got an ice cream on a trip with her, I would get the same when they returned home. I clearly remember the motto 'She who cuts doesn't choose', which was used on many occasions during my childhood. Needless to say, I developed a razor-sharp eye, which has meant that, from a very early age, I have been able to cut a cake in two pieces of exactly the same size. However, my mother's underlying sense of justice has also taught me to remember that everyone deserves fairness – not only when it comes to cake – and that people ought to be treated as equals.

MY mother taught me that everyone
I meet is as important as I am.

other people

24

AS a child, I was advised by my mother through a strange process of osmosis. Whatever the circumstances, she responded in a positive way. In my teenage years, any criticism on my part was met with the same response: 'You can find some good in everybody.' I came to understand that tolerance towards others makes life both easier and richer.

'IT takes all sorts to make a world'.

MY children would express themselves creatively, which was both delightful and embarrassing — as a teenager, our eldest son had such a complicated hairdo that he could have used his head as a serving tray for pizza. My mother never judged. She taught me that each generation has its own traits. 'I don't expect people to be the way they were when I was young,' she said.

WHEN I was six, I was so painfully shy that I could barely look at, let alone speak to, adults whom I didn't know well. But one day my mother explained that grown-ups often found it hard to talk to children, which is why they sometimes said things that seemed silly or annoying, like, 'My, haven't you grown!' It made all the difference because, instead of worrying about how shy I felt myself, I worried about how shy the grown-ups might feel of me.

other people

27

'I tell you what, Miss Lizzy, if you take it into your head to go on refusing every offer of marriage in this way, you will never get a husband at all — and I am sure I do not know who is to maintain you when your father is dead. I shall not be able to keep you — and so I warn you. I have done with you from this very day.'

Mrs Bennet in
JANE AUSTEN's
Pride and Prejudice

love and success

'DON'T worry, darling. You
can do better than that.'

'YOU'VE got plenty of time
to find the right person.'

MY mother warned me not
to trust a man with blue eyes.

MY mother used to say, 'You should always put each other first. It's good for you both and good for your children'. It was so much a part of our family culture that, when my eldest brother spoke at her funeral, he said something like, 'She had a very good marriage, and as children we knew she would always put her husband first — and none of us ever had a problem with that'.

love and success

THROUGHOUT my teens, whenever my friends and I were leaving my house to go to a party, all dressed up and feeling like grown-ups, my mum would call out, 'Don't forget your condoms, girls!' I was always incredibly embarrassed, but secretly proud that my mum was so open about being safe. My friends and I learned that sex wasn't something to be ashamed about — and we were always careful!

IN the 1950s my mother insisted, 'You must have something to fall back on' — meaning a career (in case a marriage went sour or your husband died). I think she was wistful that she didn't have training or a career of her own.

MUM used to say, 'No unwanted babies,' (that is, don't have children too young, and preferably not out of wedlock). Careers, careers, careers was her mantra.

'ALWAYS have your own bank account.'

WHEN I was 12, and we were extremely hard up, I promised my mother that I would make lots of money when I was grown up so that I could look after her in her old age. Very wisely, she said that however rich I became I would always find ways to spend money so that there would be none left over. I am still waiting to discover the truth of this.

I long to put the experience of fifty years at once into your young lives, to give you at once the key to that treasure chamber every gem of which has cost me tears and struggles and prayers, but you must work for these inward treasures yourself.

HARRIET BEECHER STOWE

strategies for happiness

'ALWAYS try to wake up with a smile
to greet the beginning of a new day'.

'SAY every morning when you get up,
"Every day and in every way, I am getting
better and better and better."'

'NEVER leave home without ten cents
and a rain bonnet, in case of emergencies.'

strategies for happiness

'JUST remember, the nicest children always belong to slightly selfish parents.'

WHEN I was a child, my mother said no plastic (Barbie dolls and the like) or bad literature in the house. How I appreciate those sentiments now, and most of what she said. Now I can even hear her when I talk to my own girls. It's really scary!

ONCE, when I was very depressed, at the age of about eight, my mother sat on my bed and said the reason I felt so bad was that I had 'an artistic temperament', which meant I was the kind of person who suffered extremes of emotion – sometimes I would feel very down but at other times I would feel ecstatically happy. This made being depressed seem an exotic advantage in life and instantly cheered me up.

'A still tongue keeps a wise head.'

MY mother taught me that — no matter how sad, scared or unwell I might feel — a good giggle works wonders. Even during the most challenging times, my mum is able to raise a laugh and make herself, and everyone around her, feel good.

'IT will all be better in the morning.'

God could not be everywhere and therefore he made mothers.

JEWISH PROVERB

domestic goddess

'THERE is no place like home.'

MY mother taught me how to make
a bed – with proper hospital corners!

THE way to anyone's heart is through their
stomach. My mum always makes time to
bake our favourite cakes.

domestic goddess

MY mother's way of teaching me how to cook a meal was brutal but effective. She had to go into hospital for a minor op and arranged that I would cook my father's supper. I was 16 and had just left boarding school to become an apprentice journalist, so I knew nothing about cooking, except for the rock-hard rock buns taught in domestic science. My mother had bought a guinea fowl. Horrified, I asked how to cook same.

'I'm far too busy now – just as usual', she said. So I consulted dozens of books and opted to cook the bird as if it were a chicken with added *gratin dauphinois* and a green salad (which I did know about). My father was delighted and I was triumphant. So much so that my mother was rather miffed. 'Well', I asked, 'how would you have done it?' 'Don't ask me, darling, I've never cooked guinea fowl before either.'

MY mother and I share a love of gardening. She taught me how to garden, and through her I have come to see how much pleasure there is to be had in watching things grow. I now get huge satisfaction from growing and eating my own fruit and vegetables.

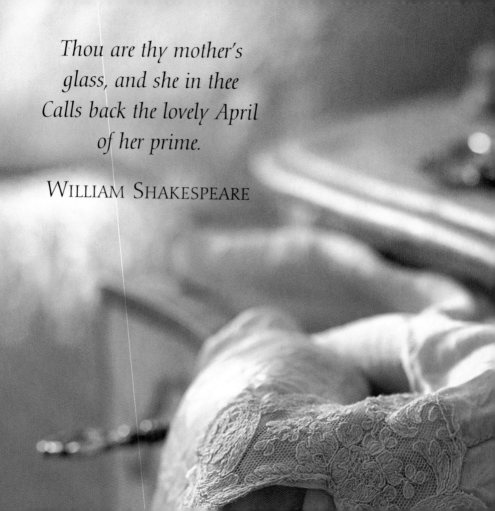

Thou are thy mother's glass, and she in thee Calls back the lovely April of her prime.

WILLIAM SHAKESPEARE

looking good

'A two–mile walk and
fresh air are imperative every day,
whatever the weather.'

'GET lots of fresh air for
a good night's sleep.'

'MAKE sure you always wear a good bra, and never leave the house without lipstick!'

'THERE'S no point in crying; it just makes you look ugly and gives you a headache. And never, ever brush your hair in public – it's revolting.'

'ALWAYS get your eyebrows done by a professional.'

looking good

'THERE'S always time to go shopping.'

'ONE never regrets extravagance.'

'SHOULDERS back, stomach in, chest out.'

'YOU can never have
too many shoes.'

'WEARING uncomfortable shoes gives
you wrinkles'. As I've never had the feet
(or legs) for Manolos or Jimmy Choos,
I can't say if it's true!

acknowledgments

KEY a=above, b=below, c=centre.

The publishers would like to thank our contributors
who made this book possible:

Henriette Bretton-Meyer, pages 22–23;
Jane Bromham, page 50b; Jessica Brown, page 56a;
Ros Byam Shaw, pages 27, 37, 43; Charlotte
Chamberlain, page 11a; Caroline Clifton-Mogg,
pages 12a, 19b, 57b; Linda Collister, page 61;
Leslie Geddes-Brown, pages 50–51; Catherine
Gough, page 41c; Judy Harrison, pages 12c, 42;

Emily Hedges, pages 10, 24, 48c, 53;
Miriam Hyslop, pages 33, 44c, 48b; Rachel Hyslop,
pages 15a, 19a, 58a, 58b; Jill Jackson, page 21a;
Camille Liscinsky, pages 26b, 41b; Stephanie
Martin, page 58c; Eliza McIntyre and
Georgia Levison, page 60; Natasha Mirzoian, pages
14, 19c, 41a; Annabel Morgan, pages 44a, 57a, 57c;
Anna Percy-Davis, pages 34b, 42b; Alison Starling,
pages 12b, 44b; Caroline Starling, page 25;
Rosemary Van Wyk Smith, page 34a; Patricia
Webb, page 31; Liz Wilde, pages 15b, 21b.

acknowledgments

photography credits

Caroline Arber, pages 1, 36; Carolyn Barber, page 14; Dan Duchars, pages 18, 30–31, 32, 59; Daniel Farmer, pages 13, 22–23, 40, 54–55; Catherine Gratwicke, pages 2, 3, 60–61; Nicky Dowey, pages 52–53; Christopher Drake, pages 50–51; Sandra Lane, pages 42–43; Emma Lee, page 35; Debi Treloar, pages 4–5, 6, 8–9, 10, 20, 24, 26–27, 38–39, 46–47, 49; Chris Tubbs, page 56; Polly Wreford, endpapers, pages 16–17, 45; Andrew Wood, pages 28–29.

picture credits

Page 10, Clare and David Mannix-Andrews' house, Hove, East Sussex; pages 46–47, Cristine Tholstrup Hermansen and Helge Drenck's house in Copenhagen; page 49, The designer couple Tea Bendix & Tobias Jacobsen's home, Denmark (www.tobiasjacobsen.dk); page 56, Mike Taitt's railway carriage in Scotland.